SUPER
SIMPLE
ORIGAMI

# ORIGAMI ZOO ANIMALS

## Easy & Fun Paper-Folding Projects

### Anna George

Consulting Editor, Diane Craig, M.A./Reading Specialist

**Super Sandcastle**

An Imprint of Abdo Publishing
abdopublishing.com

# abdopublishing.com

Published by Abdo Publishing, a division of ABDO, PO Box 398166, Minneapolis, Minnesota 55439.
Copyright © 2017 by Abdo Consulting Group, Inc. International copyrights reserved in all countries.
No part of this book may be reproduced in any form without written permission from the publisher.
Super SandCastle™ is a trademark and logo of Abdo Publishing.

Printed in the United States of America, North Mankato, Minnesota
102016
012017

THIS BOOK CONTAINS
RECYCLED MATERIALS

Editor: Liz Salzmann
Content Developer: Nancy Tuminelly
Cover and Interior Design and Production: Mighty Media, Inc.
Photo Credits: iStockphoto; Mighty Media, Inc.
Special Thanks to Kazuko Collins

The following manufacturers/names appearing in this book are trademarks: Elmer's® Glue-All®

**Publisher's Cataloging-in-Publication Data**
Names: George, Anna, author.
Title: Origami zoo animals: easy & fun paper-folding projects / by Anna George.
Other titles: Easy & fun paper-folding projects | Easy and fun paper-folding projects
Description: Minneapolis, MN : Abdo Publishing, 2017. | Series: Super simple origami
Identifiers: LCCN 2016944707 | ISBN 9781680784510 (lib. bdg.) |
    ISBN 9781680798043 (ebook)
Subjects: LCSH: Animals in art--Juvenile literature. | Origami--Juvenile literature.
    Paper work--Juvenile literature. | Handicraft--Juvenile literature.
Classification: DDC 736/.982--dc23
LC record available at http://lccn.loc.gov/2016944707

Super SandCastle™ books are created by a team of professional educators, reading specialists, and
content developers around five essential components—phonemic awareness, phonics, vocabulary, text
comprehension, and fluency—to assist young readers as they develop reading skills and strategies and
increase their general knowledge. All books are written, reviewed, and leveled for guided reading and
early reading intervention programs for use in shared, guided, and independent reading and writing
activities to support a balanced approach to literacy instruction.

# CONTENTS

# AMAZING ORIGAMI ZOO ANIMALS

Origami is the art of folding paper. In Japanese, the word *ori* means "to fold" and *gami* means "paper." People in Japan and all around the world enjoy origami.

Do you have a favorite zoo animal? Is it an elephant? Or maybe a snake? This book will show you how to make those animals and more! These super simple origami projects are great for beginners. You will learn about:

- different types of paper folds
- **symbols** used in origami **diagrams**
- types of paper that will work for origami

You'll be **amazed** at what you can make with just one sheet of paper!

# BASIC FOLDS

## MOUNTAIN FOLD
Fold behind to create a mountain.

## VALLEY FOLD
Fold in front to create a valley.

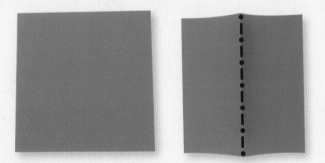

## CREASE
Fold and unfold to make a **crease**.

# ORIGAMI SYMBOLS

The **symbols** below show the most common actions used in origami.

| | |
|---|---|
| – – – – – – – – – | Valley fold |
| –·–·–·–·–·–·– | Mountain fold |
| ———————— | **Crease** |
| ⬳⟶ | Fold and unfold |
| ⟶ | Fold toward the front side |
| ⟹ | Fold toward the back side |
| ⤳ | Turn over |
| ↻ | Rotate |
| ⟼ | Pull or push |
| ———————— | Cut with scissors |

# SPECIAL FOLDS

## INSIDE REVERSE FOLD

This fold is often used to make the head or feet of an animal.
It may seem hard at first. After you practice it will become easier.
Here are instructions to make this fold.

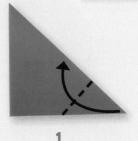

**1**

Fold a square piece of
paper into a triangle. Valley
fold one of the points.

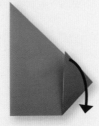

**2**

**Crease** it firmly.
Unfold.

**3**

Mountain fold the
crease. Unfold.

**4**

Unfold the paper. Place it so the
center crease is vertical. Valley
fold the bottom point.

**5**

Refold the
center crease.

# OUTSIDE REVERSE FOLD

This fold is often used to make the head of a bird or the feet of an animal. It is just like the inside **reverse** fold except the corner is folded on the outside.

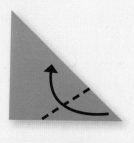

**1**
Fold a square piece of paper into a triangle. Valley fold one of the points.

**2**
**Crease** it firmly. Unfold.

**3**
Mountain fold the crease. Unfold.

**4**
Unfold the paper and turn it over. Place it so the center crease is vertical. Valley fold the bottom point.

**5**
Refold the center crease.

# BASES

These shapes are used as bases for many different origami models. Practicing these will help you improve your origami.

## KITE BASE

**1**

Place the paper on the table with one point at the top.

**2**

Valley fold the left point to the right point. Unfold.

**3**

Valley fold the two side points up to the center **crease**.

**4**

This is the finished kite base.

# FISH BASE

**1**

Start with the kite base.
Unfold the side points.

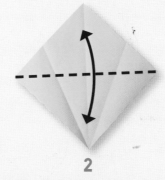

**2**

Valley fold the bottom point
to the top point. Unfold.

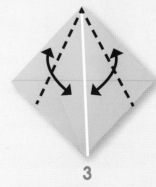

**3**

Valley fold the two side
points down to the center
**crease**. Unfold.

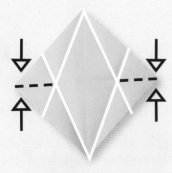

**4**

Pinch the side points into
valley folds.

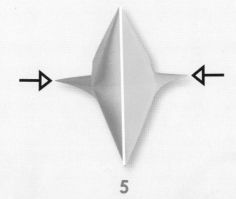

**5**

Push the side points together so
they meet in the center.

**6**

Fold the points toward
the top point. Press flat.

# MATERIALS

BONE FOLDER

CRAFT STICK

## PAPER

You can use almost any type of paper for origami. You can get special origami paper at craft stores or online. You can also use copy paper, magazine pages, scrapbooking paper, and even gift wrap!

## CREASING TOOLS

The edge of a ruler, craft stick, or bone folder can help you make good **creases** and folds.

## SCISSORS

You will need scissors if you are starting with a sheet of paper that isn't square. (See page 13.)

## EXTRAS

These are **optional** supplies used in this book.

- googly eyes
- glue
- markers

# TIPS AND TRICKS

## GET SQUARE

Many origami models use a square piece of paper.
It is easy to make a rectangular piece of paper square.

1 Fold one short edge so it lines up with a long edge.
  **Crease** the fold.

2 Cut off the strip under the triangle.

3 Unfold the paper. Now you have a square!

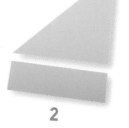

1

2

3

## PRACTICE MAKES PERFECT!

When folding origami models, it is important for the folds to be as **accurate** as possible. Match up the edges and corners when folding. Make firm creases. The more folds there are, the more important it is to make them exact. So get out some scrap paper and practice, practice, practice!

# FRIENDLY FOX

- paper (square)
- googly eyes
- glue
- marker

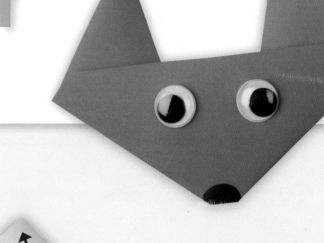

**1**

Place the paper on the table with one point at the top.

**2**

Valley fold the bottom point to the top point.

**3**

Valley fold the top point down to the bottom edge.

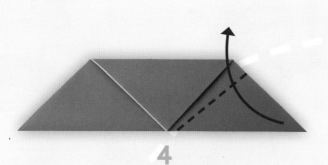

**4**

Valley fold the right
point up above the
top fold.

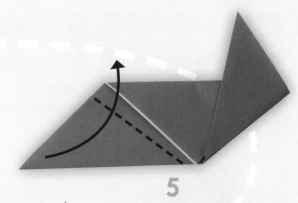

**5**

Valley fold the left
point up above the
top fold.

**6**

Turn the model over
from side to side. Glue
on the googly eyes.

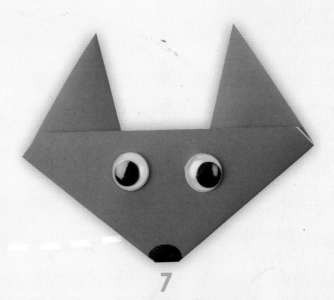

**7**

Draw the nose
with a marker.

# SLITHERING SNAKE

- paper (square)
- googly eyes
- glue

## 1

Place the paper on the table with a point at the top. Your snake will be the color of the facedown side.

## 2

Valley fold the bottom point up to the top point. Unfold.

## 3

Valley fold the bottom point to the center **crease**.

## 4

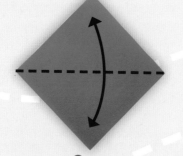

Valley fold the bottom up to the center crease two more times.

## 5

Rotate the model so the folded edge is at the top. Repeat steps 3 and 4 with the other point.

## 6

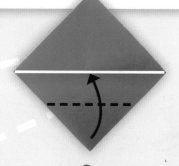

Valley fold the top to the bottom.

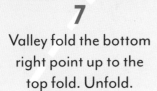

**7**

Valley fold the bottom right point up to the top fold. Unfold.

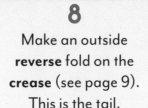

**8**

Make an outside **reverse** fold on the **crease** (see page 9). This is the tail.

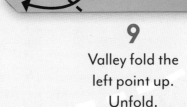

**9**

Valley fold the left point up. Unfold.

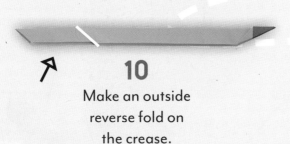

**10**

Make an outside reverse fold on the crease.

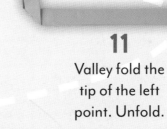

**11**

Valley fold the tip of the left point. Unfold.

**12**

Make an outside reverse fold on the crease. This is the head.

**13**

Bend the snake's body into a curve. Glue on the googly eyes.

# TRUMPETING ELEPHANT

- paper (square)
- googly eyes
- glue

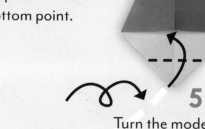

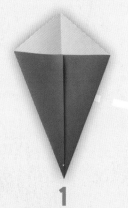

**1**

Start with a kite base. (See page 10.) Your elephant will be the color of the outside.

**2**

Turn the model over from top to bottom.

**3**

Valley fold the top point to the bottom point.

**4**

Valley fold the point back up slightly below the **previous** fold.

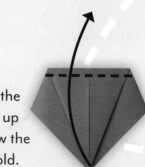

**5**

Turn the model over from side to side. Valley fold the bottom point to the bottom of the flaps.

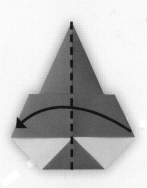

**6**

Valley fold the right side to the left side.

**7**

Valley fold the point down. Unfold.

**8**

Make an inside **reverse** fold on the **crease** (see page 8).

**9**

Valley fold the point. Unfold.

**10**

Make an inside reverse fold on the crease.

**11**

Glue a googly eye to each side of the head.

# SILLY
# SEAL

- paper (square)
- googly eyes
- glue

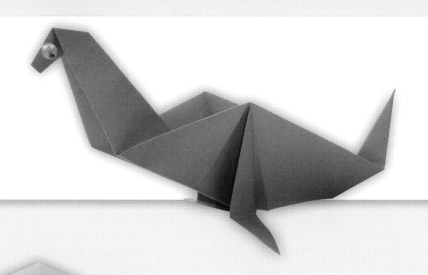

**1**

Start with a fish base. (See pages 10 and 11.) Place the base on the table with the flaps pointing to the right.

**2**

Turn the model over from side to side. The flaps should now be facedown and pointing to the left.

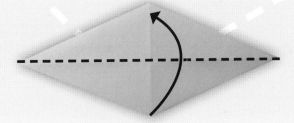

**3**

Valley fold the bottom point to the top point.

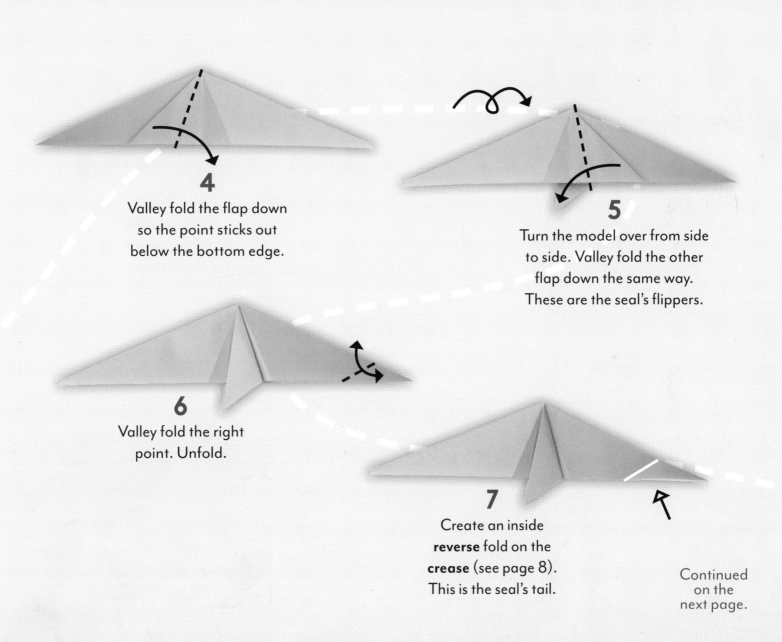

**4**

Valley fold the flap down
so the point sticks out
below the bottom edge.

**5**

Turn the model over from side
to side. Valley fold the other
flap down the same way.
These are the seal's flippers.

**6**

Valley fold the right
point. Unfold.

**7**

Create an inside
**reverse** fold on the
**crease** (see page 8).
This is the seal's tail.

Continued
on the
next page.

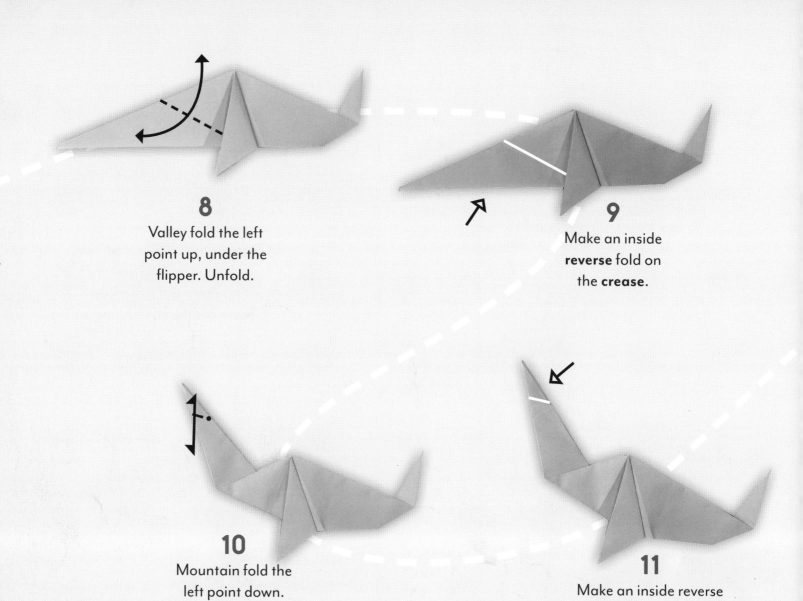

**8**

Valley fold the left point up, under the flipper. Unfold.

**9**

Make an inside **reverse** fold on the **crease**.

**10**

Mountain fold the left point down. Unfold.

**11**

Make an inside reverse fold on the crease. This is the seal's head.

## 12
Mountain fold the
tip of the seal's
head. Unfold.

## 13
Make an inside **reverse**
fold on the **crease**. This
flattens the seal's **snout**.

## 14
Valley fold each of
the flippers up so
the seal can stand.

## 15
Glue a googly
eye to each side
of the head.

# DIVING DOLPHIN

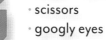

- paper (square)
- scissors
- googly eyes
- glue

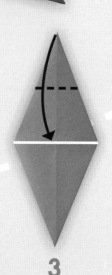

**1**

Start with a fish base. (See pages 10 and 11.) Place the base on the table with the flaps pointing up.

**2**

Turn the model over from side to side.

**3**

Valley fold the top point down to the center **crease**.

**4**

Valley fold the
same point back
up slightly below
the first fold.

**5**

Valley fold the
small points on
each side. Unfold.

**6**

Create an inside
**reverse** fold on each
**crease** (see page 8).

**7**

Valley fold the top
point about halfway
to the first fold.

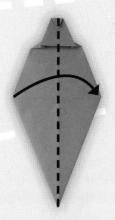

**8**

Valley fold the
left point to the
right point.

Continued
on the
next page.

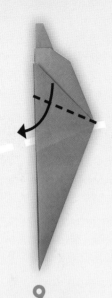

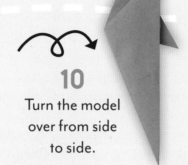

**10**

Turn the model
over from side
to side.

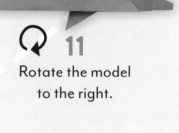

**11**

Rotate the model
to the right.

**9**

Valley fold
the flap so it
sticks out past
the left edge.

**12**

Lift and open the top flap.
Press the right side flat. Then
press the left side flat. This is
the dolphin's **dorsal fin**.

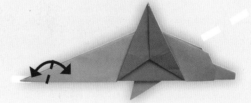

**13**

Mountain fold
the bottom point.
Unfold.

## 14
Create an inside **reverse** fold on the **crease**. This is the tail.

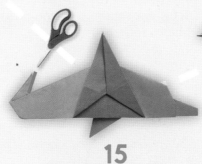

## 15
Use a scissors to cut the tail along the inside reverse fold. Unfold the inside reverse fold.

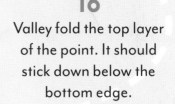

## 16
Valley fold the top layer of the point. It should stick down below the bottom edge.

## 17
Mountain fold the back layer. These are the dolphin's tail fins.

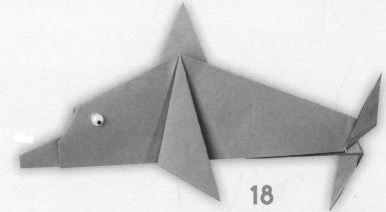

## 18
Glue a googly eye to each side of the head.

27

# STRIPED
# TIGER

- paper
  (1 orange square,
  1 black square)
- scissors
- glue
- googly eyes
- marker

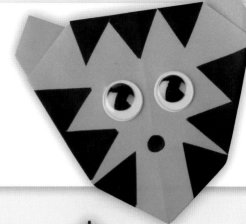

**1**

Place the orange paper on the table with one point at the top. The side facing down should be orange.

**2**

Valley fold the bottom point to the top point.

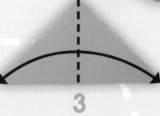

**3**

Valley fold the right point to the left point. Unfold.

**4**

Valley fold the right point. The point should stick up above the side.

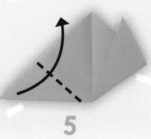

**5**

Valley fold the left point the same way.

**6**

Valley fold the center point.

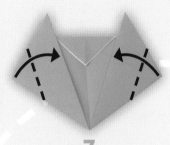

**7**

Valley fold the side points to the edges of the flaps.

**8**

Make an inside **reverse** fold on each top point (see page 8).

**9**

Turn the model over from side to side. This is the tiger's face. Set it aside.

**10**

Place the other paper on the table with a straight edge at the top. The side facing down should be black.

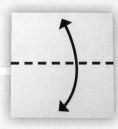

**11**

Valley fold the bottom edge to the top edge. Unfold.

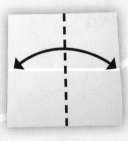

**12**

Valley fold the left edge to the right edge. Unfold.

Continued on the next page.

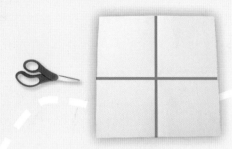

**13**

Cut the paper along the folds to make four smaller squares.

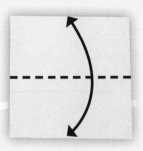

**14**

Place one small square on the table with a straight edge at the top. Valley fold the bottom edge to the top edge. Unfold.

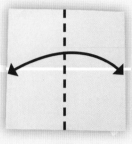

**15**

Valley fold the left edge to the right edge. Unfold.

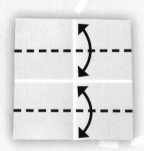

**16**

Valley fold the top and bottom edges to the center **crease**. Unfold.

**17**

Valley fold each side to the center crease. Unfold. There will now be 16 squares.

**18**

Mountain fold the top and bottom edges to the center crease.

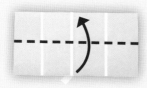

## 19

Valley fold the
bottom edge to the
top edge.

## 20

Make **diagonal** cuts
across the squares. Don't
cut all the way to the top
of the center two squares.

## 21

Unfold. Cut the
two halves apart,
if necessary.

## 22

Fold the halves around
each side of the tiger's
face. Glue them in place.

## 23

Repeat steps 14 through
21 with another small
square. Glue one half of it
between the tiger's ears.

## 24

Glue on the googly
eyes. Draw the nose
with a marker.

# GLOSSARY

**accurate** — exact or correct.

**amaze** — to surprise or fill with wonder.

**crease** — 1. a line made by folding something.
2. to make a sharp line in something by folding it.

**diagonal** — at an angle.

**diagram** — a drawing that shows how something
works or how parts go together.

**dorsal fin** — a flat, thin part on the back of
a sea animal, such as a dolphin or shark.

**optional** — something you can choose, but is not required.

**previous** — the one or ones before.

**reverse** — backwards, in the opposite direction.

**snout** — the jaws and nose of an animal.

**symbol** — an object or picture that stands for or
represents something.